Obvious words of pain, anxiety,
moping, coping and sprinkles of
hoping, but anyway
Who gives a crap?

© Hen.D.Sark

Hendsark.poetry@gmail.com

Feb 29 2020

1. Whatever
2. Spiral
3. "
4. Go away
5. Who gives a crap?
6. Down
7. Numb
8. If
9. Boo!
10. Attention
11. Dark
12. Socials
13. Brave face
14. Climb
15. Trickster
16. Locked up
17. Crap shit wee poo
18. Too much pressure
19. Snake
20. Dismiss
21. In the know
22. Droney baloney
23. It's you!
24. Aliens
25. "
26. Friends
27. Troubles
28. Selfish
29. What!
30. Think

Whatever...

My head is all wrong, wrong, wrong

I don't know what's right

I just see the crap in the world

and everything's shite

The answer to happiness . . . lies in my head

But this head is wrong, wrong, wrong

I want to be dead

I know if I end it . . I'll live it again

Can't tick off my lessons

Unless I remain

My head is all wrong, wrong, wrong

It needs putting right

But where do I start?

When I don't give a shite.

Spiral

The spiralling down was discreet

As my eyes slowly fell to my feet

While everyone else in my way

Was having a wonderful day

As dreariness crept its way in

With heaviness under my skin

Subdued in the eerie of dream

Inside I am ready to scream

Shying behind any door

Withdrawing myself evermore

The muddles inside interact

Not sure what is fiction or fact

Glancing the depth of the bin

Clinging on, holding the rim

Failing to grip anymore

Expecting to fall to the floor

If I claw my way over the waste

Staring my woes in the face

Straighten my spiritual spine

I can pull myself out just in time

I know I can climb up this pit

By tasting its tiresome grit

One day I'll be ready to soar

If I ever - get out - of indoor.

Go Away!

Don't feel like talking today
Don't feel like saying a word
Don't want to listen to crap television
or hear things I've already heard

Don't feel like going to work
Don't feel like staying at home
Don't care today, so here I will stay
And muddle around on my own

Don't feel like thinking at all
Don't feel like using my brain
Don't want my head churning guilt fear & dred
into something resembling pain

Don't want to stay or to go
Don't feel like making a choice
Don't wish to be here with you or with me & I
don't want to hear my own voice

Don't want to look at the day
Don't want you blocking my way
So, for once and for all, I won't answer don't call
and that's all I am going to say

Who Gives A Crap?

Who gives a crap?
Leave me to nap
Awesome is boresome
I know it's a trap

I see all this shit
Don't want none of it
What to enjoy?
It's a ploy and I quit

What if I'm wrong?
Here I belong
I serve a purpose
Much further along

I'll just have to wait
Search for my 'great'
Believe in myself
Or I'll die filled with hate

Down

I'm down
There's nothing here in this town.

I'm done
I cannot be bothered to run

That's it!
And really, I don't give a shit

I'm down
I don't care to turn it around

It's deep
I'd rather be falling asleep

It's low
I've been here before, so I know

It's crap
When you feel you are nothing but scrap

I'm fine
I'm not having a very good time

Numb

I feel so much, the feelings gone
NUMB
I bashed into the door, I was
NUMB
Normally I swore - still
NUMB
I didn't flinch at all as I am
NUMB

That's what I've become
. . . . NUMB

A spider crawled across my arm
NUMB
Usually I'd scream and run
NUMB
I slowly glanced its presence still
NUMB
I calmly flicked it off, I'm

. . . DONE!

If

If I do myself in, someone else will get hurt
If I drink lots off gin, I'll be on high alert

If I stay in my bed, I will struggle to rest
If I'm lost in my head, I will never be
blessed

My problems are mine, they're not going
away
Yet how do I function and get through the
day

Got pills from the doctor, I float on a cloud
They don't solve the noise as it's no longer
loud

I ache for the answer, our quests are unique
No other can help me, 'myself' I must seek

Boo!

Boo! happy happy feeling
I didn't see you leaving
Where are you, I'm grieving

Boo! happy happy feeling
The moment I need healing
You couldn't stand the squealing

Boo! happy happy feeling
Forget what I believe in
What do I achieve in?

Boo! happy happy feeling
Remember you from dreaming
What's the point and meaning

BOO!
Bloody
HOO!

Attention

Why would I need to be noticed?
When all I desire is home

Why do I need to raise the roof?
Preferring to be alone

Why should I need attention?
Anyone looking this way

Why do I need conversation?
I have nothing worthy to say

Dark

The dark, the weary and not so cheery
are coming to take me away
In my mind they seek to find my
unhappiness as prey

It can start with a sigh and a tear in my
eye
They'll swoop in and intersperse
Ever be thinking as down I am sinking
Stirring me up for the worst

Forcibly feeding me thoughts I'm not
needing
Until I'm wound up in a coil
Now I can't cope and I'm in for the
mope
Oh, what a nice day to spoil.

Socials

Socially withdrawn
I'm as forlorn as I am spent
Wrapped up in a cuddle
With my arms of discontent

Blankets, pills and chocolate
That'll block it, drown the sound
Silently its booming
Anti-tuning up and down

Slipped into a coma
Willing loner, in the way
Can't get out of bed
Then must I dread another day

Who would give a toss?
I'm no -one's loss, they cannot see
Somewhere deep inside
I need to muster up my me.

Brave Face!

Put on a brave face?
Fuck you! Fuck you!
Put on a brave face is all I ever do

Put on a brave face
Why? Why?
Putting on a brave face would mean I'd
have to lie

Put on a brave face
Yeah, Yeah
Put on a brave face? to ask me, is it fair?

Put on a brave face
No! No!
Putting on a brave face is just another
show.

Climb

My traumas are slow to burn

My lesson is long to learn

Did I *really* choose this path?

If I did, I was having a laugh

Maybe I'm living a lie

Trying my best to get by

In doing this thing that I do

Why does it feel so askew?

Trickster

Trickster got me good and proper
Cheater got me beat
Fraudulent, disorient has stitched me up a treat

Criminally, sin-ably taken for a ride
Robbed most blind came from behind
As usual they lied

Thieving, scheming, lifting, thrifting
Scumbags of the earth
Pocket picking, tricky dicking, lying shites of
worth

Sneaky takers, promise breakers, greedy needy
shifters
Bogus binding, fast rewinding
scoundrelific grifters

Super conned, aggrieved and wrong,
Bullied and annoyed
Schemed and scammed, deceived and planned,
consciously devoid

Locked Up

Locked up in a room of disbelieving

Looking through myself with eyes of pain

Coping with the life I am receiving

Living on the edge of what's mundane

Time that's on the line provokes the
meaning

Giving into what you always knew

At the station where you stop the dreaming

Grasping the reality, you grew

CRAP, shit, wee, poo.

Poems of crappy shittyness
Simple things that I address

Basic words of rhyming turds
Trapped in the winds of stress

Poems of letting it go
Flushing the 'I told you so'

Cringey rhyming and iffy timing
And written without any 'know'

So why do I put it out here?
I don't want attention or cheer

I've seen people's pain and been feeling
the same
It seems we're all one giant tear.

Too Much Pressure

I've built up the courage to say no
It's not for me or I don't want to go
No, not a killjoy or letting you down
So why the pressure to have me around?

I thought about it tiresomely
Decided that it's not for me
I knew you would try to talk me round
I'd have a job to stand my ground

Hence, I picked my words with care
Not let you in, if you should dare
But dare you did and found a clause
And here I sit, drawn in your force

My clever, polite and strong decline
Again, it hasn't worked this time
My resolve is final, that's all I know
I'm sick of the pressure, the answer is no

Snake

The word constrictor will strangle your talk
Twisting the sentence until it's contorted

Context is pointless, you don't get that far
Strike with momentum, they change where you are

Coiling round chatter whilst spinning your truth
Watching you scramble to further your proof

Meanings have stretched as they're swallowed up whole
Notions that never would come from your soul

Whatever you've said now is something anew
You're hung out to dry as the snake is now you.

Dismiss

Every enough is tough
When is enough, enough?
How many times can we redraw the lines?
Put up with crimes and stuff

When is finally done?
Never, but ready to run
How much more, is enough to ignore
Everything under the sun?

In the Know

The world is run by nasties
People in the kNOw
Signs and slippery fingers
Scraps with which they throw

It's harder to ignore them
The people in the kNOw
They infiltrate your joy
As they keep you hanging low.

They're happy, it's on purpose
The people in the kNOw
Imagine they are bogies
They're gone with just one blow

Droney Baloney

Droney Baloney
It gets in the way
The good thoughts I'm thinking
Whatever I say

Droney Baloney
So easily soothes
Ready to justify any bad moves

Droney Baloney
Will sabotage mood
Feeding me thoughts with baloney type
food

Droney Baloney
Is chaos to feel
Don't eat it, beware! step away from that
meal

It's You!

I don't feel relaxed in your company
Anxiety builds from the floor

I feel like a smell
Your nose doth repel

And a conversational bore

I wondered it may be my thinking
Picking up vibes that weren't true

But you make it heard
Without saying a word

I know I'm not wrong and it's you!

Aliens

Cruel and confusing they bite as they fly
Throwing themselves in your face
Frantic you brush them away, or you try
but sticky they are to embrace

They don't have to roam as they know when
they're home
the sight of you clear in their view
The one very reason that they were all grown
Is so they would end up on you

Choosing to wear them, they'll use you as food
Spiking your blood as they bite
Eating away as they bring down your mood
as hours do pass you in spite

Throwing them back, it isn't much fun
as more will be born on the double
Getting caught up in their numerous sum
will only bring more of the trouble

Dodging will only buy you some time
They'll follow you, all of your days
Knowing they're there but pretending it's fine
Will poison your innocent ways

Verbal attacks whether true lies or facts
Imagine your ears have been burning?
Digest and release them, don't fester to please them
Much better to be un concerning

Forgive and forget, they were never a threat
when caught with those gossip delighters
Their shtick throwing war won't be fought anymore
when care not, for those wordpool igniters

'Friends'

I can't say no to some people
Some people do worm their way in
I know that I come across feeble
And always go out on a limb

Excuses I'd make for protection
No unwanted 'friends' at the door
They'd never stand up to dissection
I'd still end up doing the chore

I've tried to say no and not waver
Steadfast unwilling to bend
But then I'm called out for behaviour
On not being nice to a friend

I'm happy to give what I want to
Convenient offer of time
Some people suck out all your kindness
They're taking the piss out of mine

Cutting them off isn't easy
They don't go away on their own
The only release that can free me
Is blocking them off on my phone

Troubles in my tummy slowly
form
Bubbles in the brain are being
born
Rubble in my throat are
piercing silent hands that
choke
And all because I have to leave
the home!

Selfish?

Selfish I am doing all that you say
As I follow your plans
Your decisions all day
I've something in mind
For myself, should I say?
I'd like to do 'this', but we don't go that
way

Selfish I am as I'm told to comply
I do as you ask,
I don't need to try
It's easy to please thee
Just ask for the sky
I'm selfish that way, so you say, don't
know why?

What!

Times flown
Moneyblown
Budgettough
Feelingrough
What to do?
Nothing new
Here ♡ before
Know the score
But Not today
Not going that way
Woes be small
Be Changing it all
So, No more pain
Let's Stop this game
Just for me
Let me be

Think

I thought about it once
I thought about it twice
Now I'm thinking constantly
I can't put it on ice

I have to think about it
It's always on my mind
Growing ever bigger
I can only see behind

I have the choice to dwell,
Linger and assume
Keep the living hell
Or light up like the moon

Like

I really don't like you today
You're moody and making me pay

It hurts when you shout and go on
It's funny how you're never wrong

We can't have a quiet debate
If not your decision – you hate

The only thing here I can see
Is today you didn't like me.

Out Tonight

I'm out tonight
Arranged for a while
I don't want to go
So forcibly smile

I'm out tonight
I bubble inside
It pops in my chest
I wish I could hide

I'm out tonight
Why such a wreck?
Invisible hands
Are gripping my neck

I'm out tonight
I'll make myself known
I'll give it an hour
Then I'll come home

Call Off the Dogs

Oh no! bad show! what have I done
Got in a mood and spoiled the fun
Spoke out, there's no doubt. I'm way out of
line
Gobbing off, kicking off at the wrong time

The people, the steeple, all know what they
saw
They're looking at me like I started a war
I'm sure someone else was the first to
declare
But I came along and I took it from there

Don't want to reflect & I don't need
reminding
I analyse me and I'm constantly finding
I'm flawed and imperfect, I learn by the
knocks
For now, I'm so sorry. Please call off the
dogs.

Help!

Could you understand the feeling
of needing to be held?
So much desperation
but oh so deaf and proud

Do you ever feel so lonely
when life looks like it's well
Wanting some attention
yet scared as hell to tell?

Could you understand the feeling
you need someone so much
You only have to call them
but you failed to keep in touch

Do you ever think that someone
the closest person who
Should know when you are needy
and shake you out the blue?

Will

Where there's a will there's a way

But Will isn't willing to play

Will has gone fishing

Can't feel my heart wishing

Not hearing a word that I say

I depend upon Will, for surviving

Will is direction and driving

Will's on a woe

Its answer is no

I don't know why Will is depriving

Where is the way without Will?

When Will is so quiet and still?

Will's not behaving

Won't answer my craving

I wonder if Will could be ill

Me

Piecing together the meaning of me
The meaning of life
The nonsense it be

All that I am, all that I do
What got me here
I haven't a clue

All the woes, I never address
The shocking mistakes
That led to success

Behind interaction, paving the way
Tomorrows reaction?
My feeling today

Hurt

Hurtful words from others, we can choose
whether to listen

Hurtful words from us are more dangerously
given

Just because another person wants to put us
down

It's up to us to let them in, why do we give a
damn

To choose retaliation whether rightly justified

We let ourselves become like them, our
goodness is denied

Forgive

Don't want to say sorry, forgive and forget
This wasn't my doing – I have no regret

I must have got lost in your negative hue
I'm guilty of nothing, the fault lies with you

Yet whilst I am justified, rightfully pained
No-one else knows, and I'm still being
blamed

Don't want to defend or pretend it's ok
On doing so, people throw doubt in my way

I know if I let go forgive and forget
Try to get by and to cross off the debt

I may be aggrieved while relief can be slow
I'm freeing myself when I let that shit go

Judgement Day

Judge and jury, what say you?
Are you judging?
All I do?
It's not just me, there's others too
Judge and jury
What say you?

Judge and jury, what's the game?
Am I playing?
What's the aim?
Don't judge others, spite or slay?
And *do* that always, everyday?

Judge and jury, still you dwell
Raining on me, bloody hell
Why the victim, why choose me?
It's in my head? How can that be?

Judge and jury, what say thee?
I judge myself! The judge is me?
Resides inside my being - bare
It cannot lie, it's always there

Judge and jury, what say you?
Everyday this play I do
Whatever is my truth today
Tomorrow is my judgement day.

Let Down

I let you down last minute
Ignored your reaching out
I didn't bother listening
Or giving you a shout

I just became reclusive
Locked into a zone
Feeling such a nuisance
Pottering alone

I never meant to hurt you
Or push you far away
With lots of thoughts to think through
I don't know what to say

Disappointing

Disappointments *my* feeling. not theirs
They may be the ones – who acted unfair
Whatever their reason, they're gone
Now out of sight, yet I ponder on

Disappointment is mine – to keep
Whatever the reason, if it runs deep
Here I am feeling the bite
Whilst here they should be, putting it right

Disappointment, why do I hold on?
It may be my right but it's doing me wrong
I'm worried that if I forget
They're getting away without showing respect

Disappointment I want you to know
It's hard, I've decided, I'm letting you go
You're being replaced with content
Whilst taking away this lesson for which you
were meant.

Tick

One day at a time they say
But hours they get in the way
When down, out and lonely
Time passes so slowly
One minute seems like a
whole day

The Truth with A Tail

The truth with a tail was no friend
They told their truth with a bend
Not quite the full story
Yet told in full glory
For chaos around to descend

The truth with a tail was unkind
The truth with a tail wasn't blind
They clearly could see
that by telling on me
I would look bad in everyone's mind

Think on, when you're telling a tale
On a 'bad to serious' scale
If it's nothing at all
and it's whimsically small
Then it's really not worth the betrayal.

Letter

I'm sending a letter
An honest account

My bitter emotions
I'm writing them out

After its posted
And found my address

I'll set it on fire
And sweep up the mess

Heavy

Instinctively I want
Yet logically I weigh
Myself - I watch them both
I choose which to obey

Weight is sometimes heavy
My logic gives me grief
Instinctively it tilts for me
I choose the quick relief

If weights and wants were balanced
After watching them debate
My choices would be clearer
& my head would be my mate

?

I don't know where to begin
Don't want a fight
Don't need a win

All has already been said
It may not be right
It's how it's been read

I don't know where I should start
How hard can it be?
To open my heart

Where is the line I should stand?
With nothing but love
I offer my hand

Little Sentence

One little sentence from my mouth unto
your ears
Repeated unto others over coffee, lunch
or beers

Idle chatter, spiteful natter, any shape or
form
Building up momentum, heavy
pressure, due a storm.

Innocent our voices as we waffle all day
long
Little do we know, that seed we sow is
growing wrong.

If we took the time, to check our head
before we speak
We'd get along so nicely and we'd have
a cracking week

Amiss

Somethings amiss
Don't know what it is
A yearning desire
A smallness so bliss

I look, I am searching
For what? I don't know
Frustrated I am
I ache as I go

I ponder, I wonder
Its stirring within
Tapping my shoulder
and not giving in

A whisper of wind
No direction to blow in
Won't be revealing
So, no way of knowing

Would Love

I would love to love having some fun

I would love to know *what* fun to have

Would love to be carefree and run

Would love an address for the cab

Would love to know which way to go

Would love to get lost in some wishing

Would love to know what *is* to know

Would love to know what I am missing

Hmmm?

Decision to make
Which road should I choose?
I cannot decide
Which is win? which is loose?

Where should I be?
Where should I go?
Should I ask someone else?
Better they'd know

Wisdom inside
Where do you hide?
If only I knew, what to do
I'd abide

Choose I must
Be grateful & trust
Abandon my thoughts
Having never been fussed.

Sticks and Stones

Somebody threw me a word
I felt perturbed
Was it to spite me?

Words with intention to maim
Drive me insane
Served up to fright me

A whirlwind of worry does spin
Settle within ___
Pondering over

Boring its way through my head
Seeing it red
Gone supernova

That's when I stop and say NO
Let the words go
Shoo them away

Words, they disperse on their own
Not welcome home
Get on with my day

What I Am Not

I won't feel bad that I'm not yet wise
Whilst living a life, I get many tries

I won't feel bad if I'm not as clever
I am what I am and that's whatever

I won't feel bad if I don't look the part
I can change what you see by using my
heart

I won't feel bad about what I've not got
I can get by ok, without needing a lot

I won't feel bad to be judged with scorn
We're all the same, we've all been born

Blame

No one to blame but self
I did it myself with my mouth

No one to blame but I
I felt it yet I don't know why

No one to blame even so
I did it but I didn't know

No one can change what I see
So, see how I want it to be

Self-Pity

Self-pity, you're shitty and I got you beat.
Can't fettle to settle, you end in defeat
I don't entertain with your troublesome score
It's not being played like it used to before

Self-pity, you're gritty, yet I know your ploy
Hypnotic you seep in, yet quick to destroy
Whatever my troubles, I'll think on them pure
With you they turn toxic. Don't need that allure

Self-pity, you're witty but try as you like
I'm guarding my mind so piss off, on your bike
Whatever my harm is, I'm calm, and I rule
Stop hanging around. I'm no longer your tool

Self-pity ain't pretty, attractive or fun
It renders me useless, pathetic and numb
I won't be a part of that scene, no siree
Self-pity, who are you? You're no part of me.

Scream !

at the top

of my voice

I don't have a
Choice

Inside, seeing
'something'

Change my scream
to a sigh
Wave it
goodbye
It might become

NOTHING

3 Wise Monkeys

3 wise monkeys said to me
Don't Talk
Don't Listen
Don't you See

Disappointments, Disagree
Monkey Mind
Won't let
Me be

3 Wise monkeys set me free
Don't Talk
Don't Listen
Don't you see?

I Am

My eyes don't see what you see
My ears don't hear the same

My words are planted in me
I am what I became

My thoughts are what I make
them
My worlds inside my head

My feet walk where I take them
I am all I have said

Figment

Who plants the nasty in my mind?
Who gives me thoughts that are unkind?
Who plants the worry, fear, the trickster to my
soul?
Who plays the dark side in my role?

Who stirs me up when I'm confused?
Who makes me rake up old bad news?
Who keeps me in the thoughts I'd rather have
set free?
Who pulls me down when I am me?

Who - Isn't her or him or me
Who - Needs a name, what can it be?
Who - Isn't friendly, loving, honest, nice or kind
Who - Is a figment of my mind

Who is the 'me' that knows it's wrong?
Who wants that figment to be gone?
Who - Me? - We're not the same, there's two
of us in here
Who let that figment in my ear?

Wise

Are you or me, the same as we be?
Ten or fifteen years ago?

Are we now different in that which we see?
With matters we did not then know

Our we not growing our own separate trials
Nourished, neglected or blessed

Why to suppose then, all types, shapes and
styles
Are equal to know what is best

Whatever I used to think, what I know now
Forgive me - my old thinking ways

I've grown up a little, wiped sweat from my
brow
And learning tomorrows new days

Say What?

Somebody threw me a word
Flipped me the bird
Objected my space

Blood pumping filled with defence
Clouded my sense
Screwed up my face

Words began flying like spears
Stinging the ears
Causing offence

Actions unworthy to share
People were there
Feeling it tense

As did the drama unfold
Story was told
Gathering flair

All because of a word
If I hadn't heard
Or chosen to care

Flip

I'm feeling very low
and I know
I need to Flip it

My situation here,
What's the fear?
Can I flip it?

Yet at this point in time
I'm not fine
I'm a mess

I'm dwelling on a 'thing'
What it brings?
Unhappiness

I want myself to care,
Life ain't fair
What's the meaning?

Shouldn't I feel 'this'?
What it is
I am feeling

Yet all it does is hurt
in the dirt
Stop the pain!

Don't want to be asleep
fall in deep
Wax and wain

Whatever I am thinking
When I'm sinking
in this pit

What's the other side?
Exactly opposite
this shit

Flip this things direction
In that section
of decision

Maybe it's a lie
but I'll get by
with better vision

Better

There's always someone better than me
Doing what I do best

Perhaps I should do it anyway
See if I progress

I don't know why I'd bother
I only offer less

There's always someone better than me
I'll never be the best

Lucky

Someone is more successful than me
Yet I am so much better

How can I accelerate
And be like that go-getter

Maybe they are lucky
They can write a better letter

Probably conspiracy
or karmical vendetta

Mindset

Someone else is coining it in
Whilst I am earning nil

I could do it blindfolded
But no one knows my skill

On paper I'm a nothing
I have no grades to fill

If only I had confidence
I Know I would be brill

Others

Someone else is different than me
They'll always be someone else

I can only be my me
When looking on myself

By watching all the others
I'm giving up on wealth

No self-love or kindness
Isn't dandy for my health

Don't get mad get even

The worst thing ever heard

Mad is mad, but scheming?

Now who is the turd?

No Harm

With no harm to others
I do as I dare
I'll never be nasty
Don't want to go there

With no harm intended
I do as I can
Neutrally equal
I am what I am

With no harm not ever
I do as I die
Helpful and giving
I'm free to go by

I'm In Charge!

I'm in charge of what I think about
Feel it good and make it lovely
Thinking thoughts that I could do without
Cast them out and rise above thee

I'm in charge of all I dream about
Eyes are wise, feeling wholesome
Squish down thoughts I ought to be without
Weed them out, before they grow some

I'm in charge of all I focus on
Make it fun and play it thoughtful
Drifting thoughts will take me where it's wrong
Pay attention where I ought to

I'm in charge of every thought I sow
Think up scenes and dreams of good stuff
Doubt and fear are not the seeds to sow
Take control, the heads enough.

Happy

Today I'm feeling happy
I want the world to know
I'm driving in my car
I'll let the other drivers go
The ones who take advantage
They don't bother me today
I just behave the way I feel
- Lovingly in play

People who are in a mood
They want to gripe and moan
Have no patience, no sensations
Thoughtfully unknown
I let them win, don't get drawn in
It flies above my head
Giving them no meaning
Means bad feeling won't be fed

I'm not a mat to tread on
Yet I'm noticing it's wise
To pick my battles carefully
Proportionate to size
Abstaining from the dramas
Popping up throughout the day
Ignoring all the boring
Un-inviting it to stay

Light

I love the light, It's airy and bright
Seeing is easy. So clear is my sight

Dark is dense. It comes at expense
The feeling is heavy. I stiffen and tense

I love the light, Try as I might
It poses a challenge I need to get right

Darkness peers. It brings with it tears
Creeping up slow to entwine with my fears

Lightness shines through cracks and lines
Lifting me higher for happier times

with dark dispersed I'm over the worst
Bright is the light as it quenches my thirst

I'm Mindful of My Actions
I Utter Not Absurd

To Value Interaction
Is to Value Every Word

Bad

Bad knows love, if it loves what it does

Bad can't last, if it's put in the past

Bad can change if it's love can be gained

Bad gone Good,

Oh, I wish, wish it would

Love

Love is not a choice it is the reason

The only test we're given is to love

Every act against love is a daemon

Only pure of heart can rise above

Past can be forgiven if you mean it

Keeping up the good is our endeavour

You cannot lie inside or try to scheme it

It's only when you love you're living clever

I'm Trying My Best

Straighten my back, it's good for my spine
Talk calm and softly, most of the time

Conflict is teacher, I use what I learn
Nip the buds early then show no concern

Always begin with a friendly approach
In disagreement I am my own coach

Emotions inside can be hard to supress
Many a trigger will find my address

Hold a calm nerve whilst biting my tongue
Whatever it takes is how it is done

If someone is bossing or giving me grief
It may be a test of my newfound belief

Yet challenged I weep or fiercely defend
It's up to me now I decide how I bend

Once in the moment I may become weak
Hooked in the clutches of terrible speak

Pull myself back and remember my quest
I'll kick myself later, I'm trying my best

Healthy heart
Healthy mind
Loving each
and every kind
Having faith
Loving true
Oh, how lovely
Lovely you

END GAME LAW

Financial Mindset in Quotables

CHARLES MWEWA